P9-EED-355

vitality

home spa
vitality

Jo Glanville-Blackburn

RYLAND
PETERS
& SMALL
LONDON NEW YORK

In memory of my mother Margaret Patricia Glanville-Blackburn.

Designer Sarah Walden
Editor Miriam Hyslop
Picture Researcher Emily Westlake
Production Tamsin Curwood
Art Director Gabriella Le Grazie
Publishing Director Alison Starling

First published in the United States in 2003
by Ryland Peters & Small, Inc.
519 Broadway, 5th Floor
New York NY 10012
www.rylandpeters.com

10 9 8 7 6 5 4 3 2 1
Text, design, and photographs
© Ryland Peters & Small 2003

ISBN 1 84172 380 0

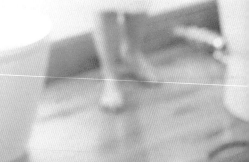

If you are in any doubt about your health, please
consult your doctor before making any changes to
your usual dietary and wellbeing regime. Essential
oils are very powerful and potentially toxic if used
too liberally. Please follow the guidelines and never
use the oils undiluted on bare skin, unless advised
otherwise. This book is not suitable for anyone
during pregnancy.

A CIP catalog record for this book is available from the
Library of Congress.

Printed and bound in China.

contents

introduction

We all need a little more vitality in our lives—in our bodies, our hearts, and our spirits. Creating a spa within the home is about making it easy for yourself, for home is where you can—and must—make the time to energize yourself inside and out. Here you can enjoy the comfort and security of your personal space to try something new, learn a fresh technique, or even just think about something in a different way.

Don't feel you have to do everything. There's no pressure here. Choose your time, then plan a little ahead so you have everything you need to hand—fresh fruit and vegetables, your favorite music, warm clean towels, your favorite bath oils, a cozy pair of slippers. Above all, make your spa inspiring—a place where you want to be. That way, you will find yourself there more often.

So whenever you are feeling tired and need reviving— in the morning, throughout the day, or just before an evening out—there is something here for you to enjoy now, and build into the rest of your life.

"In the race to be better or best,
do not miss the joy of being."

Anon

"Happiness is not a destination. It is a method of life."

Benton Hills

wake up

fresh start

Begin your spa day in a brighter, more positive mood with one or all of these energizing body boosters that you can do today and every morning of your life:

Try a little light therapy. Welcome the morning sun when you wake by throwing back the curtains. When sunlight enters the retina of the eye, it inhibits the release of melatonin (the biorhythm hormone that makes you sleepy), boosting your energy levels and mood.

Take a big yawn ... or two. It's your body's way of getting more oxygen to the brain, and increases mental clarity at the same time.

Practice better breathing. It clears the head, helps you focus, and reduces stress. Breathe in as slowly as you can (try to count as far as ten), then breathe out equally slowly.

Why not sing in the shower to lift your spirits? Music brightens your mood by tuning in to the right side (the creative side) of your brain.

awake your senses

Start using your senses to give you renewed energy.

SMELL Aromatherapy is the fragrant mind and body therapy that uses the aroma of essential oils to heal everyday ailments and influence emotions. Essential oils are easily absorbed through the skin, directly into the blood-stream, and as a result are considered extremely powerful. (Never use them undiluted on your skin.) The easiest ways to use the oils are: diluting six drops in a warm bath or sprinkling them in the shower tray before you turn the water on; diluting five drops in two teaspoons of sweet almond oil for massage; inhaling them from a tissue, or using them in a room vapourizer.

Five of the best energy boosting oils:

Uplifting **BERGAMOT** lifts the spirits to relieve depression, melancholy, and general fatigue.

Reviving **GINGER** massaged over the kidney area will revive vital energy.

Detoxifying **JUNIPER** a stimulant and diuretic, is also great for eliminating toxins from the body.

Invigorating **LEMON** lifts the spirits, boosts the immune system, and is perfect first thing.

Stimulating **ROSEMARY** raises energy levels when you are stressed or tired.

SEE & FEEL Color therapy changes our moods and can give us energy. It works on the colors of the seven "chakras" of the body—also the colors of the rainbow. Eat, wear, and see **RED**, which affects the adrenal glands, to boost willpower and vitality; **ORANGE**, which affects the reproductive organs, to increase happiness and optimism; and **YELLOW** for the pancreas, to increase alertness.

HEAR Music is cleansing and uplifting to the body. Research shows that it boosts the immune system and reduces stress. "Music has vibration. It resonates and cleanses through the body," says aromatherapist Noella Gabriel. "Your favorite piece of music is therapy for you in its own right."

TASTE Flower essences are designed to treat emotions and balance out negative feelings. To add vitality, try **HORNBEAM** for that "Monday morning" feeling or procrastination, **OLIVE** for exhaustion, **WILD OAT** for general apathy and lack of drive, and **LARCH** if you're feeling underconfident.

energize within

The way you think and feel about yourself every day, from the moment you awake, affects your vitality from within. Those of us who develop a positive mental attitude to life are more successful, happier, and healthier. But it starts with you: you need to love yourself before anyone else can.

When you look in the mirror in the morning, try this **POSITIVE MIND EXERCISE**. Gaze with your right eye into the reflection of your left eye while silently giving yourself positive thoughts (called affirmations). This helps to boost the creative side of your mind. Next, focus on the space between your brows (this is the positive you—the third eye—which brings enlightenment). Stroke this area and visualize doing all you need to do in order to follow through your affirmations.

brighten up

1 Replace your morning coffee with a cup of hot water and two slices of fresh lemon.

2 Eat protein for breakfast to boost your brain's levels of dopamine and make you feel alert as well as keeping your blood sugar steady.

3 Finish your morning shower with a cold burst of water for two minutes to boost your circulation.

4 Stress dispels energy fast. 10–20 minutes of deep breathing and relaxation will help invigorate mind and body.

5 Mix two drops each of lavender and peppermint oil in two teaspooons of almond oil. Rub into neck, temples, forehead, and earlobes, to brighten your eyes, clear your mind, and relieve a headache.

6   When you feel sluggish, eat foods such as spinach, bananas, onions, garlic, grapefruit, and pears, which cleanse your liver and eliminate toxins.

7   A daily supplement of Coenzyme Q10 provides the spark for energy production in all your body's cells.

8   Eat an orange. Vitamin C helps combat anxiety and lowers stress hormones. One orange provides the RDA of 60mg and is the perfect midmorning snack.

9   Fit in a brisk 15-minute walk. Any activity that improves circulation will boost vitality.

10   Siberian ginseng is a vitality tonic and provides an energy boost, helping your body cope better with stress.

detox

"We should all have more respect and reverence for our body. We alone are responsible for it— and its wellbeing."

Noella Gabriel

aquatherapy

For instant vitality—immerse yourself in water, inside and out. Water is the elixir of life and makes your spirits as buoyant as your body. But even though the body is 75% water, it is rarely kept topped up. Plenty of fresh, pure water daily helps the kidneys function, preventing the buildup of everyday toxins, and reduces stress, anxiety, depression, and joint pain.

introduce a little aquatherapy into your daily routine

DRINK MORE WATER It is essential for clear skin and bright eyes, and helps reduce fluid retention. Don't wait until you're thirsty—aim to drink around 3 pints (1.5 liters) of bottled water daily.

Make your **SHOWER** a revitalizing way to recharge your senses first thing in the morning. Sprinkle six to eight drops of stimulating rosemary pure essential oil in the shower tray, turn on the water, and step in. Enjoy the burst of freshness that will invigorate your body from toe to top.

HAVE A VITALITY BATH Add 2 pounds (1 kg) of Epsom salts to your bath. Don't skimp on the amount. You may feel vaguely floppy at first, but it feels wonderfully restorative.

thalassotherapy

Spa treatments have offered a cure for mind and body for centuries. Seawater is believed to have many healing properties, and adding dead sea salts and seaweed-based products to your beauty regime helps to rebalance the whole body, due to their high mineral content.

After a bath, create your own **SPA TREATMENT** with the shower. Change the water temperature to warm or cold, then spray vigorously with each setting for 10–20 seconds. Alternate six times. Finish with a warm spray for a few minutes. Pat dry and moisturize.

Imitate the **SITZ BATH TREATMENT**. Place a bowl of cold water in a warm bath and place your feet in the cold bowl, with the rest of your body in the warmth. If you can fit, swap over and sit in the cold with your feet in the warmth. This shocks the system into self-cleansing.

body tonic

A positive boost for your body—and how you feel about it—is simply to give it extra attention. When you use a body oil or cream, choose it because you love the smell of it and its texture as you massage it in. That in itself will make you feel more nurtured and uplifted.

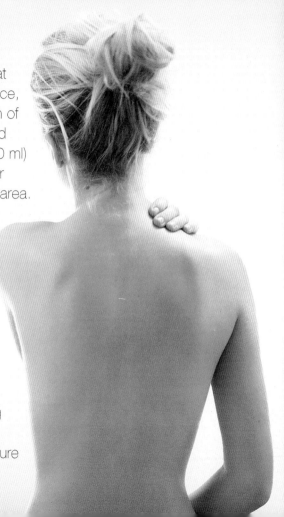

For a **TONING MASSAGE OIL** that makes a heavenly fragrance, too, mix three drops each of juniper berry, cypress, and patchouli oil with 1 oz. (20 ml) of carrier oil. Pay particular attention to hip and thigh area.

MASSAGE YOUR BODY using your knuckles for an invigorating pick-me-up. Smooth a light film of oil all over your body, then work it in using long sweeping movements from hands and feet up toward the heart. Then massage by making small circles with your knuckles. Keep the pressure firm to feel energized.

juicing

A delicious and fun alternative to eating a bowlful of raw fruit and vegetables is to juice them into a healthy drink. Eating only raw fresh fruit and vegetables up until lunch helps the liver's detoxification (cleansing) process, which is most active between midnight and midday. Avoiding other foods during this time can quickly boost the body's natural cleansing process, and a day's fresh juice fast is extremely detoxifying. The more cleansed your body feels, the lighter and more energized you will feel.

fruity taster

2 apples
½ mango
1 orange
¼ banana
1 passion fruit

Serves 1

Peel and chop the fruit. Put all the ingredients
in a blender, blend until smooth, and add
water to taste.

Remember, the riper the fruit, the more
energizing antioxidant vitamins and minerals
you will consume. Try your own fruit and
vegetable combinations.

diet

Make small changes to your diet today and you will quickly find you have more energy.

Eat a good, varied, **HIGH-PROTEIN** diet rich in vitamins and minerals. Choose power snacks such as Brazil nuts (rich in vitamin B1 and magnesium) and almonds (high in zinc, magnesium, and iron).

Eat **COMPLEX CARBOHYDRATES** such as whole-wheat bread and wholegrains, but avoid single carbohydrates such as sugar, white flour, and rice.

Try **"FOOD COMBINING"** to aid digestion, especially if you tend to retain fluid and feel bloated. As a general rule, never mix protein and carbohydrate in the same meal.

Eat **FRESH RAW FRUIT & VEGETABLES** whenever you can. Otherwise, lightly steam or grill them in olive oil.

Try to eat **THE RIGHT FATS**. Use olive oil and flax oil, as opposed to soft margarine, low-fat spreads, and butter.

eat for energy

1   An apple a day is detoxifying—a great antioxidant and full of vitamin C to keep cholesterol levels stable.

2   Avocado is high in polyunsaturated fat to keep skin soft, and it boosts metabolism.

3   Fresh nuts (almonds, hazels, Brazils, pinola, and chestnuts) are high in protein, so good for fatigue, and essential fatty acids to keep skin soft.

4   Garlic boosts cell renewal. It is antibacterial, antifungal, and antiviral.

5   A good palate and liver cleanser, lemon helps thin the blood.

6 Carrots are high in betacarotene, which is great for a healthy liver.

7 Oily fish (salmon, herring, mackerel) are loaded with essential fatty acids which fight fatigue and boost circulation.

8 Kiwi fruit is high in vitamins C and E and potassium, making it good for moods and digestion.

9 Sesame seeds are high in B vitamins, zinc, and potassium, and help keep the liver and kidneys healthy.

10 Yogurt helps to detoxify the system, promotes gastro-intestinal health, and enhances the absorption of B vitamins.

For better body
awareness, you need
to create a better
body regime for you.

rituals

revitalizing facial

Start your day with this invigorating facial.

First thing in the morning, before you apply any skincare product, **SPLASH** your face repeatedly with clean warm water to help stimulate the circulation.

Pat skin dry, then apply an invigorating face mask with uplifting ingredients such as **PEPPERMINT**, **CAMPHOR**, and **MENTHOL** to brighten the skin and the senses. Follow with a refreshing spritz of **ROSEWATER**.

Next massage your skin with a little **AVOCADO OIL** or your usual moisturizing cream. Use your fingers to gently work over pressure points between the brows, at the temples, along the jawline, and on the earlobes. This works muscles in the face, removing signs of tension.

scrubs

The easiest way to quickly revitalize your skin is to exfoliate. It removes dull, dead skin cells from the surface to reveal fresher, brighter skin beneath. You can use a dry towel, loofah, bristle brush, or scrub.

DRY SKIN BRUSHING is an intense form of exfoliation using a soft, natural bristle brush on dry skin. It not only exfoliates the skin; it improves circulation and lymphatic drainage at the same time. Start from the soles of the feet and the hands, and gradually work up the body toward the heart.

A **SALT & OIL BODY SCRUB** is a wonderful ritual to add to your vitality regime and makes you aware of your body before you even shower. It gently but thoroughly exfoliates, leaving skin silky soft, and replaces your body's natural oils with mood-enhancing essential oils of your choice.

To make an **INVIGORATING SCRUB** mix two drops each of menthol, lavender, and grapefruit essential oils in a 1 oz. (20 ml) blend of sweet almond and grapeseed oils. Add a handful of salt from the kitchen. Keep in a jar.

mud

Renowned for its deep cleansing and purifying benefits to the body, mud has long been used as a basic spa treatment. It contains many minerals, which are therapeutic for healthy skin.

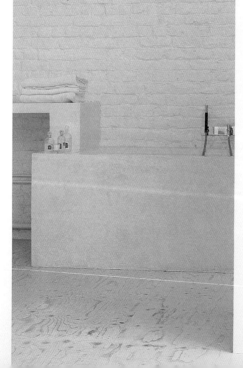

Try a **MUD BATH** at home. It can be messy—but incredibly therapeutic. Mix Fuller's earth with warm water until it is muddy, but not runny, climb in, and soak for 15 minutes. Repeat every two to three days for a couple of weeks.

A **FACIAL CLAY** or **MUD MASK** is purifying and deep cleansing, too. Leave on for 5–10 minutes; wipe off with a damp cloth, and splash with fresh water to remove any residue. Follow with a moisturizer.

hair treatments

Make shampooing your hair
a pleasurable experience.

Start by giving yourself a **SCALP MASSAGE**. Sit down, close your eyes, lean forward, rest your elbows on your knees and place your fingertips in your hair. Gently massage your scalp, being aware of gently rubbing away tiny bits of tension. Do this for 5–10 minutes; then gently lift and pull the hair up away from the scalp for a count of three. Repeat.

Give your hair a **DEEP CONDITIONING TREATMENT**. Focus on rinsing the scalp well (shampoo that hasn't been rinsed out properly is a major cause of scalp irritation). Choose a rich intensive hair moisturizer that needs to be left on for several minutes. Wrap your hair up in a warm towel to help totally smooth the hair strands. Wait for a further 10 minutes before styling your hair.

feet treats

GIVE YOUR FEET A FACIAL Use an exfoliating scrub around the soles of the feet, heels, and toes. Rinse off and soak your feet in a bathtub containing a few drops of peppermint oil to refresh and relax them. Pat feet dry and use the edge of your towel to push back the cuticles. Apply your favorite moisturizing face mask all over your feet (they need a treat, too) and put them up for 10 minutes. Wipe off any excess, spritz with a cooling toner, pat dry, and massage in a little oil around the cuticles, heels, and any dry areas.

Kick off your shoes and **WALK BAREFOOT** around your home as often as possible—it's very therapeutic.

energize your eyes

Try these quick revitalizing eye tips.

Keep your eyes feeling bright by storing your favorite **EYE CREAM** in the refrigerator so it's always icy cold when you pat it over tender, tired, puffy eyelids.

Look for eye products containing **EYEBRIGHT**, an herbal remedy that naturally constricts the blood vessels, soothing sore irritated eyes, relieving redness and tiredness. Drink the tea, take the drops, or make a soothing solution from the tea.

EYELASH CURLERS help to curl the lashes up and "open up" the eye.

"PALMING" is a gentle pressure massage to stop puffiness. With fingers pointing up toward the top of your head, gently press the heels of your hands on the tops of your cheekbones. Rest the palms gently on the eyelids so you feel the heat they generate.

quick vitality

1 Run your wrists under cold running water to boost energy levels and calm you down when you are feeling overexcited.

2 Use a water spray to revive your skin, your makeup, and your senses, anytime.

3 Add a little salt to 2 inches of cold water in the bathtub and swish your feet through as if you are wading in the sea.

4 Wear an uplifting aromatherapy blend as fragrance, rubbing it on pulse points and around the nape of the neck to pick you up.

5 Make skin look radiant: choose and use a vitamin-C face cream that brightens up dull, tired skin.

6 Pressing along the length of each brow, starting from the inner corners, stimulates the acupressure points and makes your eyes feel more alert.

7 Wear lilac eyeshadow. It immediately lifts and brightens the eyes and suits all eye colours.

8 For a quick fix, soak and chill two camomile teabags (used ones are fine), lie down, and place them on closed eyelids for 10 minutes.

9 Caffeine produces a burst of adrenaline, putting our bodies out of balance and using up endless amounts of energy. Change to uplifting herbal and fruit teas such as peppermint, fennel, and licorice.

10 Lie in a warm bath and sip ice cold water—the effect is very uplifting and cleansing.

restore

"We cannot hold a torch to light another's path without brightening our own."

Ben Sweetland

revitalize your mind

It seems illogical that using up precious energy through exercise gives you more vitality, but exercise increases blood flow and volume, strengthens your heart and lungs, and lowers your resting heart rate. All this helps you to accomplish daily activities with less physical effort and fatigue. Take up yoga, t'ai chi, Pilates, and other mind and body workouts for more energizing forms of exercise.

move

Gentle stretching has restorative powers, will quickly boost your oxygen intake, and leaves you able to relax and concentrate better. Try to fit one of these quick stretching exercises into your time. Breathe out as you stretch.

LIE ON YOUR BACK flat on the floor, with your feet together and knees slightly bent. Place a hand under the hollow of your back. Using your abdominal muscles, press your spine against the floor until your back is flat. Relax and repeat.

GET ON ALL FOURS (like a cat) with your hands and knees apart. Arch your back gently and push your head down so you feel a stretch from neck to tail. Now raise your head as you relax your back into its normal position. Repeat once.

energizing exercises

1 Plan a 10-minute peaceful walk—alone—in your day. We rarely give ourselves this time and space to think.

2 Fast walking burns more calories than slow jogging.

3 Stop the daily grind. Boredom and a repetitive lifestyle curbs vitality. Don't be a slave to routine.

4 Practice visualization: positive mental images that have a positive effect on mind, body, and spirit.

5 Declutter the rooms you live in for a calmer, more energized environment. Keep fresh air circulating and the temperature between 65° and 75°F (19-23°C).

6 For a quick facial exercise, keep your facial muscles relaxed, and make exaggerated vowel sounds (A, E, I, O, U) with your mouth.

7 Keep rose quartz at hand: in your pocket, around your neck as a pendant, or by your computer, to absorb negative energy.

8 Identify what you love about your life—and keep reminding yourself.

9 Surround yourself with people who make you feel good; they will feed you positive energy.

10 Spend more time around young children. Learn to play again, and have more fun.

Find your zest for life. Be more spontaneous. Seize the day. Forget your usual routines for the morning—the day—or the weekend. Doing something pleasurable for yourself will give you a new sense of vitality. Always seek the positive, the fun side of life. Learn something new. Have fun. It's your choice. Decide now to live a little ... or a lot.

useful addresses

Complementary Therapies:

Institute of Complementary Medicine
t. +44 (0)20 7237 5165 for details on complementary therapies.

The Society of Teachers of the Alexander Technique
t. +44 (0)20 7284 3338
www.stat.org.uk

Aromatherapy Organisations Council
t. +44 (0)20 8251 791 2
www.aocuk.net

Cariad Aromatherapy
104 Bancroft
Hitchin
Herts SG5 1LY
UK
t. +44 (0)1462 443518
Essential oil suppliers.

Stockists and Suppliers:

Aveda
t. 866 823 1425 for stores
www.aveda.com

Bed Bath and Beyond
410 East 61st Street
New York NY10021
t. 800 462 3966 for stores
www.bedbathandbeyond.com

Crate&Barrel
650 Madison Avenue
New York NY10022
t. 800 967 6696 for stores
www.crateandbarrel.com

Origins
www.origins.com for stockists & stores.

Sephora
1500 Broadway #300
New York NY10036
t. 877 737 4672 for stores
www.sephora.com

Neal's Yard Remedies
15 Neal's Yard
Covent Garden
London WC2H 9DP
UK
www.nealsyardremedies.com
for stockists & stores.
Natural health retailers.

Useful Reading:

Aveda Rituals by Horst Rechelbacher (Ebury Press, 1999)

The Spirit of Yoga by Kathy Phillips (Cassell & Co., 2001)

credits

Key: a=above, b=below, r=right, l=left, c=center

David Montgomery 1-3, 11 **br**, 12-13, 15, 20 **l**, 21 **br**, 28, 29, 33 inset **l**, 38 **al**, 38 **bc**, 39, 44, 45 **main**, 45 **inset a**, 46, 47 **l**, 52 **r**, 53 **al**, 53 **ar**, 56, 57.

Chris Everard 6 **a**, 11 **bl**, 17 **b**, 24 **al**, 24 **r**, 26, 36 **al**, 37 **r**, 38 **ar** 38 **br**, 41 **al**, 41 **cl**, 47 **br**.

Andrew Wood 4-5, 8 **bl**, 11 **ar**, 17 **c**, 21 **ar**, 37 **l**, 40, 42, 43, 45 **inset b**, 50, 51.

Christopher Drake 21 **bl**, 22, 23 **al**, 23 **bl**, 60, 61 **cl**, 61 **cr**.

William Lingwood 6 **b**, 18, 19, 30, 31, 34, 35.

Polly Wreford 16, 17 **a**, 48, 49 **inset**, 53 **br**, 59, 63.

Henry Bourne 24 **bl**, 27, 32, 41 **r**, 64.

Caroline Arber 7, 20 **r**, 38 **bl**, 41 **bl**.

Debi Treloar 49 **main**, 54-55, 61 **l**, 61 **cr**.

Alan Williams 10, 11 **al**, 11 **bc**, 58.

Jan Baldwin 8 **al**, 23 **ar**, 25.

Tom Leighton 9, 33 **main** & **inset r**.

Chris Tubbs 8 **ar**, 23 **br**, **endpapers**.

David Brittain 14, 52 **l**.

James Merrell 47 **ar**.

Ray Main 62.

The publisher would like to thank all the homeowners and designers who allowed us to photograph their homes and work.

acknowledgments

The author would like to thank the following for all their help in the making of
Home Spa: Vitality:
Fiona Lindsay of Limelight Management and Alison Starling of Ryland Peters & Small
for making it happen; my husband James Stanton for always running the bath;
Noella Gabriel, aromatherapist and Director of Product and Treatment Development
for Elemis for her wisdom; Glenda Taylor, aromatherapist for her encouragement;
nutritionist Ann-Louise Gittleman for her endless advice; and Reiki healer
Mark Hegarty for his focus.